Raptors
Birds of Prey

LEVEL  READER

READING LEVEL
3
GRADES 2 TO 4

Copyright ©2011 Dalmatian Press, LLC. All rights reserved.
Printed in China.

Written by Kathryn Knight
Illustrated by Edizioni Larus S.p.A. and Sabrina Marconi

The DALMATIAN PRESS name is a trademark of Dalmatian Publishing Group,
Franklin, Tennessee 37068-2068. 1-866-418-2572.
No part of this book may be reproduced or copied in any form without written permission
from the copyright owner. CE13854/1210

DalmatianPress23401095BF16842264-03/11

Raptors

Speed. Power. Keen eyesight. Terrifying talons. These are the marks of some of the fiercest hunters on Earth—the raptors. Raptors are birds that prey on other animals, even other birds. Eagles, hawks, falcons, owls, and vultures have large talons (claws) and strong, hooked beaks that rip and tear.

The name raptor means "one who seizes or takes by force." Raptors have incredibly good eyesight. Some can spot an 8-inch object from two miles away.

Most raptors hunt while soaring on their long, broad wings.

Golden Eagle

Nicknamed the King of Birds, the golden eagle is one of the best-known raptors in the world. It is named for the golden feathers on the back of its head. These powerful birds can have a 3-foot body length and a 7-foot wingspan. They prey on rabbits, small mammals, reptiles, birds, foxes, goats, and even young deer.

Raptor Nests

Most raptors build nests, but some "borrow" nests made by other birds or animals. One desert hawk nests in a hollow cactus. Other raptors simply lay eggs on a cliff or building ledge.

The largest raptor nests are built by eagles. Using twigs and leaves, eagles add to their nests year after year. These nests can grow to 4 to 9 feet across.

Some eagle nests are up in high trees. Many are built on cliffs. An eagle nest is called an *aerie* (**air**-ee).

Bald Eagle

The bald eagle lives only in North America. It is a large, handsome bird with a 7-foot wingspan. With expert timing, it swoops down from a tree and grasps a small mammal or fish in its talons.

The male and female build an aerie in the branches of a tall tree or on a cliff. They take turns hunting and caring for their two eaglets.

African Sea Eagle

This majestic raptor soars over lakes and rivers of southern Africa. It is related to the bald eagle. It feeds mainly on fish, and is also called the African fish eagle. Its strong wings allow it to fly with a 3-pound fish in its talons. With a heavier fish, the eagle may "paddle" to the shore using its wings.

Osprey

The osprey (**oss**-pree) is a fish-eating raptor found nearly worldwide. It is also called a sea hawk. Ospreys have unusual talons. Like eagles, they have four toes. Unlike eagles, which have three forward-facing toes, ospreys have a movable outer toe. Ospreys are able to grasp prey with two toes in front and two behind. This is very useful in catching slippery fish.

Eagle Owl

Many raptors are *diurnal* (daytime) hunters. Owls are *nocturnal* (nighttime) raptors. Owls have large eyes with keen vision. They glide silently on broad wings looking for rodents, small mammals, and reptiles.

One of the largest owls is the Eurasian eagle-owl. This powerful raptor can have a 6-foot wingspan. The eagle-owl has a call that sounds like *oo-hoo*.

Snowy Owl

Perhaps the most beautiful owl is the snowy owl. Males are pure white with yellow eyes. These large raptors blend in with snowy landscapes of the far north. Unlike most owls, snowy owls hunt day or night.

These birds often make a nest on the ground or on a large flat rock. The female lays 5 to 10 eggs. Both the male and female care for the chicks.

Vulture

Birds of prey are excellent hunters. Some raptors, however, feed on only weak and dying animals. Some are scavengers, feeding on *carcasses* (bodies) of animals already dead. The largest scavengers are the vultures. These magnificent birds soar on wings that can span 7 to 10 feet. Some stand 3 to 4 feet tall.

The Egyptian vulture
is clever. It is one of the
few birds that will use a
"tool." It uses stones to
break eggs.

Old World vultures of Africa, Asia, and Europe are closely related to eagles and hawks. They spot carcasses mainly by sight. New World vultures of North and South America include condors and turkey vultures. Unlike other raptors, they have a keen sense of smell. Some New World vultures can smell a dead animal from as far away as a mile.

Andean Condor

   The males of many raptors are smaller than the females. However, the male Andean condor is larger than the female. It is one of the largest flying birds, standing over 4 feet tall and having a 10-foot wingspan.

   Andean condors will prey on animals, but they mainly scavenge for carcasses. They glide for hours on *thermals* (currents of heated air) high above the Andes of South America, looking and smelling for food. Once a condor begins to feed, it is soon joined by fellow condors to share in the feast.

Harpy Eagle

The largest, most powerful eagle in the Americas is the female harpy eagle. The harpy eagle is named after the monstrous harpy of Greek mythology, which had a woman's face, huge claws, and a vulture's body.

Harpy eagles mainly prey on animals that live in trees, such as sloths, monkeys, opossums, and birds. These eagles are incredibly strong. A 20-pound harpy eagle can carry a 14-pound howler monkey!

Raptor Wings

    Raptors display amazing flight skills. Some soar for hours. Some dive with incredible speed. Some can dart around trees while chasing prey. Many raptors can soar, dive, and swoop along the ground, catching prey completely by surprise.

    Long, broad wings allow large raptors to stay aloft on updrafts of air. They can even "float" high above the ground without flapping their wings for up to 20 minutes.

The short, broad
wings of hawks
and owls enable
them to make
sharper turns
as they go
after a meal.

The diving masters of the raptor world are the osprey and the falcons. Their long, narrow, pointed wings turn these birds into speeding arrows as they plunge toward prey.

Peregrine Falcon

The fastest animal is the peregrine falcon. These birds are built for speed. They have long, pointed wings and a long, narrow tail. When a soaring peregrine falcon spots a meal, it pulls its wings in tight and dives straight for its prey at up to 200 miles an hour!

Great Horned Owl

Hoo-hoo hoooo hoo-hoo. If you hear this call at night, it is probably a great horned owl. These large raptors are the most common owls in the Americas. Even with a wingspan of 3 to 5 feet, their flight is silent. A great horned owl can swoop right next to you, and you might never hear it.

Little Owl

Kee-ik. Kee-ik. That's the call of one of the smallest owls: the little owl. In Greek mythology, these 10-inch birds were sacred to the goddess Athena.

Goshawk

A fearless, aggressive hunter inhabits the
northern forests of the world. The goshawk is
a handsome raptor with long legs and talons and
great speed. Its wing shape allows it to zip around
trees in pursuit of birds or rabbits. It will even
chase prey into the underbrush—on foot!

Philippine Eagle

The Philippine eagle is one of the largest and rarest birds in the world. This majestic giant only lives on a few forested islands of the Philippines, and females lay only one egg each breeding season. The male and female bond for life—and that can be for a long time. Philippine eagles may live 30 to 50 years.

Philippine eagles are the main predators on their islands. They are very powerful hunters, preying on small to medium-size mammals, reptiles, and birds. Although they are huge birds, they are quick and agile—and smart. A pair of Philippine eagles will sometimes team up to hunt a troop of monkeys. One will sit on a perch to get the monkeys' attention, while the other swoops in to grab one.

Smaller Raptors

Some of the more colorful and spirited raptors are the sparrowhawks, merlins, kestrels, and falcons. Though not as powerful as eagles, vultures, and large owls, these small hunters are no less fierce.

Sparrowhawk

Rodents, small lizards, birds, and insects are easy prey for these swift flyers. Many hunt while hovering above the ground. One quick, steep dive—and those talons are grasping a meal.

Merlin

Smaller raptors can be found worldwide, mainly in forested and grassland areas. Some, like the Mauritius kestrel, are rare and live only in one area. There may only be 1,000 Mauritius kestrels left on a few Pacific islands. Others, like the common kestrel, are widespread across a few continents.

Mauritius kestrel

Common kestrel

The smaller raptors are often more colorful than the larger raptors. Merlins have striking blue feathers. Kestrels may be a rich cinnamon-brown or blue-gray with a blue cap.

Lammergeier

The lammergeier (**lam**-mer-gye-er) is also called
the bearded vulture. It lives in high, rocky, mountainous
areas, scouting for carcasses. But it is not after the meat.
This massive bird feeds on the marrow in the bones.
It can swallow whole bones, but it prefers small pieces.
A lammergeier will grasp a bone, fly to about 200 feet in
the air, then drop it onto a flat rock, shattering it. It will
also seize smaller prey, such as turtles,
to drop in the same manner.
These bone-loving birds
will even knock a larger
animal from a cliff.

Burrowing Owl

The tiny burrowing owl can dig its own home, but it prefers to "borrow" burrows from other animals, such as prairie dogs. These long-legged little birds live in grassland and desert areas of the Americas, where their *hoo hoo* call can be heard day or night. They feed mainly on insects and small rodents.

The cute, curious burrowing owl has a flexible neck. It will tilt and turn its head upside down to focus on an object.

Like other owls, the burrowing owl can turn its head to look backward.

Secretary Bird

The most unusual raptor is the secretary bird of the African savanna. It has a long tail and the longest legs of any raptor, making it the tallest bird of prey. Secretary birds have soaring wings, but they prefer to hunt on the ground, looking for insects, small mammals, and reptiles—particularly snakes— to eat. They often kill with a swift kick, then rip and tear their prey—like a true raptor!

Its head-feathers look like the quill pens that clerks or secretaries would hold behind their ears— hence its name.